SO, YOU THINK YOU KNOW
HOW TO
STUDY?

Tyrone L. Bennet, Ed.D

Printed in the United States of America

ISBN: Softcover   978-1-63871-211-4
        eBook   978-1-63871-212-1
        Hardcover   978-1-63871-213-8

Republished by: PageTurner Press and Media LLC
Publication Date: 05/19/2021

To order copies of this book, contact:

PageTurner Press and Media
Phone: 1-888-447-9651
order@pageturner.us
www.pageturner.us

SO, YOU THINK YOU KNOW HOW TO STUDY?

Tyrone L. Bennett, Ed.D

Foreword

If you are ready to take the next steps to make a brand-new start in your studying habits whether good or bad you need to make a choice. But first let's look at a few reasons why you are in this predicament that lead us to help you resolve the problems in the first place.

Looking at where we are today in our nation's education system, the high school graduation rate showed about 69.7% of students from the age of 16 to 24 have graduated and enrolled in college from January to October 2016. The actual numbers were about 3.1 million in that age group.

According to the Center for American Progress, the United States has 60% of its students taking remediation classes in English, math, or both. It is no secret that America's educational system has its flaws. Too often, our educators debate on what standards are best for our youth and why it's important to provide the best education for our nation's future.

If you are willing to do what it takes to learn and learn how to learn about studying, then you will be successful after these strategies and techniques are implemented.

Dedication

To my mother Janie A. Bennett who survived this horrific pandemic and continues to inspire me to do more and share the knowledge to as many students as possible.

To the thousands of students I had the pleasure of tutoring, taught and transformed their lives since 1998 in the areas of STEM, mentoring and inspiring.

I found several thought-provoking questions in a Quora.com article that was so intriguing to this topic about studying and why there are student issues and/or problems.

Those questions were as follows:

- *Should we force students to study for hours instead of encouraging them to actually practice the subject material?*

- *Why are some students better at studying than others?*

- *Why is it important for students to study seriously?*

- *If you don't study well now, what will happen in your future?*

- *Why don't students study?*

- *Are you attending class and reviewing course materials regularly?*

- *Do you organize yourself?*

- *Are you listening...or just hearing?*

- *Do you take notes or just pass notes?*

- *Does your mind wander or do you have a grip of your wandering mind?*

- *Why do students procrastinate?*

We will not attempt to answer these questions, but I would like you to think about these questions and write your own answers as you read and learn from this book. This, believe it or not, will give you an opportunity to place your own opinion on what has become a serious issue in your life as a student. Many students are feeling the effects of being unprepared in schools or training institutions. It is mostly because of the lack of preparedness and learning how to study. Many have failed in doing it or never knew how to do it well.

I often tell students that "no one knows you better than you." Parents might know their kids, but the reality is that students too often like to make up their minds about tasks and do what it is they want to do but fail to see the importance of staying on top of the task to see it through successfully.

Case in point, when a student is supposed to be studying for an exam or test, how many times do we find this student cramming for his or her exam and rarely prepared properly? According to the Association for Supervision and Curriculum Development (ASCD), many students develop poor habits and set bad behaviors. As authors of Habits of Mind, the ASCD has developed sixteen icons that spell out the habits set by student behavior. The ASCD contends that students need to practice these habits in order to be successful in a classroom environment but also should use these elements for life.

For the purpose of this book, we are going to look at six of the sixteen habits of mind indicators, namely:

1. *Persisting*

2. *Listening with understanding and empathy*

3. *Thinking and communicating with clarity and precision*

4. *Thinking interdependently*

5. *Finding humor*

6. *Remaining open to continuous learning*

These six habits of mind, I find, are essential to students and adult learners as they encounter these habits in a learning environment. The other ten are nothing to look down upon, but these are much more to the scope of this book than the others. As educators, we must provide opportunities for these students to plan for, have access to, and reflect on their thoughts and explicitly be aware of how important it is to be able to think and do it logically.

This model described and created by ASCD gives us the opportunity to be the stimuli for student development. All students learn differently and come from a variety of backgrounds. Schools should continue, as they are mandated to, to collect data on their students as they relate these habits should they pursue further analysis or assessment in their school districts.

Persisting

It is often said that "winners never quit and quitters never win." Although this may be true, everyone is given a second chance to improve his or her performance. A second chance is given mostly by those who can be persistent in their efforts toward success. If you cannot activate your will to want to do something productive, you will not succeed no matter the urge and time spent. Being persistent is fundamental after the start. How often do we find students start a goal plan and then stop that goal plan because of something like a boyfriend, a girlfriend, money, bad friends, bad choices, procrastination, or the like, which kept them from staying focused? Trust me, we all have been there at some point in our lives. Life does get in the way, but it is important to know that nothing from nothing leaves simply nothing. Am I right?

However, if you start from nothing into something, then make the best of it so your time isn't wasted. Remember, if you waste time, it is just as bad as annihilating the efforts of progress; so don't start an objective or task for success and then stop or quit before the success train arrives. If you oblige yourself to this failure preference, then you are just as bad as the next procrastinator who wakes up in the early morning hours saying, "I'm going to go to the baseball field and do the best sports performance for the team possible" but never turned in his or her try-out application. If you are going to be anything, be persistent and see how far progress can make your day much more profitable, but never allow negativity rascals to put you off your objective goal plans. It can cost you a lot of money and time and more importantly, your life will be wasted, and you will not achieve success. Many students drop out of schools, whether middle, junior, or high school.

In the year 2012 statistics, more than 1.5 million students drop out of high school in the United States each year. This is very disturbing, but more importantly, it shows how many students aren't persistent in their objective goal plans. Yes, people do have various circumstances that lead to them to drop out of school, and we do know there are many levels and issues out there that could be justified. However, young people in this country often feel they are in the know-it-all mode.

You would think as a nation we're in good shape to compete globally, but any rational person would review the facts before stating their opinion. According to a new study reported by the Business Insider, in 2018, the U.S. ranked 27th in the world for its levels of healthcare and education. This was a huge decline from decades ago in 1990 when the USA was sixth in the world.

Listen, only a fool would say, given the choice for survival, "I'd rather drink a tall glass of liquor each day for four years than a glass of water for four decades." Many young people strongly feel they know more than the senior citizens, older adults, and/or those who have over sixteen years of education under their belt. Have you ever heard of students who are very outspoken and talk back harshly to their parents and/or older adults? Many of these students are just wet behind the ears, so to speak, and haven't experienced life as we know it, but they can tell you all about the world and its problems they can solve.

Young people should understand the simple things in life especially when it comes to common sense, and they are the following:

- *Listening vs. hearing*

- *Age group and generation gaps*

- *Knowledge vs. intelligence base*

- *Wisdom and knowledge*

Listening with Understanding and Empathy

The problem we see among thousands of young people is that they don't know the difference between listening and hearing when a command is given to them for either instruction or statements to support their desires. Listen, according to the dictionary, means to pay attention or take note. The key words here are to pay attention. Hearing, on the other hand, means to perceive sound. Too often, young people do not want to take heed to those meanings.

Listening with understanding and empathy can go a long way if we pay attention to where we want to go and the path to get there in one piece. Listening gives you the instructions that follow after what it is you heard. Age groups and generation gaps are too often blamed for why many kids today don't show respect to their seniors. The idea many teens have is that they feel they are going to live forever and that they see themselves as going to live into old age. There is a generation gap.

The generation of old had the best of everything, including the good, bad, and indifference; but what they never took for granted is the respect toward seniors and the "least ones." For whatever reason, many of today's youth have lost or never had the desire to respect elders. The notion of saying "yes, sir" or "yes, madam" is not on their mind. It's sad but true. I remember a kid not too much older than me during my teens who wanted a job but refused to show respect to a construction man who was the owner of a construction company. The man told the teen that if he wanted a summer job, he must first acknowledge him as sir when talking. The teen looked at the other three people in the lobby of a six story building and thought about what was asked of him and refused to honor the man's request. He preferred showing off to his peers than being polite. He had this so-called tough-guy image, which means he should not humble himself to anyone because it would supposedly injure his ego or manhood.

It was the highest level of ignorance I have ever witnessed. Of course he did not get the summer job, but once again this example proved how our teens back then are no different from many urban and/or inner-city teens today if they don't show respect and honor their elders. There is an age group that has fostered the subject of our day.

For example, in this twenty-first century, young and old are interested in rap music. The generation gap was mended by rap music and jazz, but at the same time some "old cats" will teach young folks how to use the old styles of music like jazz and blend in the new to make a sound that renders uniqueness. Listening with empathy is not too harsh of a task to ask teens. Empathy when applied is the psychological identification with or displaced experiencing of your feelings, thoughts, or attitudes toward another. Most people are guilty of using this noun as a tool to manipulate for selfish gain. However, it should be understood that we as humans should show concern toward the feelings and thoughts of our fellow humans. The human desire should focus on getting along and/or living in peace.

Thinking with Clarity and Precision

As human beings, we think with our brains. Later on in the book, we will talk about the brain in-depth; but when you begin to think, it should be understood that thinking is something that is transported from outside yourself and bestowed inside of you. It's something God of the universe or the world gave you the power to receive. Some say it could be by accident in some way. Some people get lucky; others don't. By contrast, clarity isn't something that comes from outside of you. Clarity isn't a matter of luck either. Understand that clarity is what you create for yourself. Therefore, clarity is a decision you make. As you read this book, whatever degree of clarity you happen to experience right this minute is what you've decided to create for yourself. Understand that not deciding still counts as a decision. You deciding not to decide is a decision to remain undecided or uncertain. The word decide comes from the Latin word decidere, which means "to cut off from." To make a decision, you must cut away any and other things or potential directions. It is when you remain consistently open to lots of different directions at the same time that people get confused and fuzzy. Only when you focus on one specific direction can clarity happen.

Think about the time when you had various tasks or things to accomplish that your level of clarity wasn't the same each time. During many points in your life, you've been very clear. At other times you've been extremely undecided or uncertain. Take a moment right now and think about those times when you've been at one extreme versus the other in decision making. See if you can remember some of the underlying factors on both sides of the coin.

Thinking Interdependently

No matter who you are in this world, when you are born, you have a few things that will cross your mind interdependently; and one of those things is the idea of feeding yourself or being hungry and food must be given. Babies are a prime example of this. When they are hungry, they will cry. Any time of the day, babies will place everything in their mouths because they know that feeding the body is important. It becomes an interdependent thought. At times we all are guilty of some form of interdependent thinking. Albert Einstein once said, "Any man who reads too much and uses his own brain too little falls into lazy habits of thinking." It was Johann Wolfgang von Goethe who said, "Thinking is easy, acting is difficult, and to put one's thoughts into action is the most difficult thing in the world." I will say this: we have more time to do nothing but less to be meaningful when you waste your time thinking about what not to become. Shakespeare once said about thinking, "It is neither good nor bad, but thinking makes it so." Lastly, one of the best quotes I heard on this subject came from President Lincoln who said, "When I get ready to talk to people, I spend two thirds of the time thinking what they want to hear and one third thinking about what I want to say."

Finding Humor

What's so funny? Why laugh it off? People have been doing and/or asking these questions for years, and many have not debated the subject in recent days. Humor and stress have been going on for years. Humor is the best medicine when all other remedies, for pain relief, fail. It is well documented that using humor relieves stress or using humor has been proven to relieve stress. Unfortunately, few of us would admit we don't have a good sense of humor. Many people have lost the desire to laugh and in some cases don't find time much in our days to laugh about. With the high unemployment rate, students dropping out of schools, teenage pregnancies on the rise, and politicians lying when in office, why laugh when so much nonsense and lunacy of life is around us?

You don't have to be a stand-up comic to dazzle a group with side splitting one-liners to make humor work for you. Here are some ways you can make humor one of your stress-reducing tools: Anything that can evoke a smile can change your mood for the better. Exaggeration is another great way of diffusing a potentially stressful situation, robbing it of much of its impact. One form of exaggeration is the blow-up technique. Here's how it works: Suppose you're angry because your neighbor has the TV volume turned up too loud. Let your imagination take it from there. Now imagine that he has turned it up full blast. Not only that, but he has turned every radio he owns up to ear-splitting levels. You notice that you hear live music and realize a high school band is practicing in his living room. The walls are now shaking. You get a phone call from your cousin half a mile away, asking what's going on. The police and fire department start arriving . . . and then you smile.

Remaining Open to Continuous Learning

Keep yourself in the know. Never lose the desire to want to learn and allow ignorance to cripple your thoughts. The ASCD is an organization that encourages learning and supplies so much information for the sake of learning and being educated. What is meant by continuous learning? Continuous learning is the ability to apply strategies and support your learning with the ability to adapt to change. This is an acquired skill, and we use it on a regular basis in our workplace or with our co-workers. It can be enhanced through training in the workplace or off-site. I strongly feel that if you don't have the joy to learn continuously, then you have no strong desire to read.

Reading is not just fundamental, but it is a skill needed to recognize words, decipher words and structured sentences, and make meaning out of those sentences in order to be understood and translate information from those words created for use. At work, at play, or in any social gathering, people need reading skills to gather and use information. The information can come from social media in the form of text messages, safety instructions, hazard dangers, memos, procedure manuals, reports, media articles, proposals, and other written materials. So, students, please read! Not only is reading an essential tool and skill needed, but we should also have the love for thinking.

Thinking is a skill that involves mental processes. The reliable skill in thinking uses cognitive functions that enable people to make reasonable and logical decisions. These decisions can also be based upon critical thinking, problem solving, organizing tasks, and using a huge amount of memory to synthesize and analyze information.

Remember, thinking is a skill that is needed to remember things that are important and find information. Therefore, if you have the desire to continuously learn, you will find that thinking becomes all too necessary of a skill required to have during that process. In addition, continuous learning involves responsibilities so that you don't fall too far behind in up-to-date information. There is the idea of staying abreast with the latest in research and technology.

You must be able to capitalize on the learning process to stay trained and pursue new developments in your profession or job-related field. You can never be too old to learn. Learning is or should always be the thing to do as you grow older. It was important for our forefathers to introduce the constitution with the sight of our nation being a society of educated leaders and innovators for the future of our children.

Staying in an education mind-set is very important in my household and should be in yours no matter your status. On a personal level, continuous learning becomes essential when you begin to expand skills and skill sets through increasing your knowledge base.

Case in point, as our lives change, the need becomes more apparent for us to adapt both professionally and personally. On a professional level, continuous learning becomes essential when you desire to further expand your skill set in response to new developments in your industry or environment. Case in point, if you need to respond to changes at work with a new computer system and software, training is required to make your job more efficient.

Lastly, it is essential to continuously learn from the individual level to practice our daily routines and increase our knowledge base on the following:

• Asking for help when you don't know something

• Observing and learning from others around you

• Trying something new and making it work in a different way

• Practicing and repeating what you already learned

The attempts of fixing our nation's school system since 1964 have not been a walk in the park. Several legislations and laws have been reformed to improve ways to implement the improvement plans in our school system. Looking back at the anatomy of our education system in the last fifty years brings up very few solutions as to what direction is righteously affordable for the next generation. Whether you talk about equality of education or legislation for the common standards for K–12, it really matters if growth among the youth meets the requirements needed for the workforce to be competitive globally.

Sure, we can argue whether our youth can make it through high school, but too often we have seen large percentages of students dropping out of school across this country. In the last decade, No Child Left Behind (NCLB) was not the best attempt to improve our nation's failing schools, but it stirred the pot. Now with the impious, as some states argued, of common core standards, it leaves many other nations to wonder where do we go from here. The nineteenth-century focus in STEM progressive movement from World Wars I and II to the proliferations of drugs, sex, music, and the love of sports that have been dominating our mainstream as we struggle in the twenty-first century. The struggle of solving our failing schools and slowly increasing the readiness skills for the workforce can put this country on edge if we are to regain our might in the global market.

Policy and law makers debated the effects of the NCLB legislation. The requirements to meet Adequate Yearly Progress (AYP) have been a great challenge to low-achieving school districts and poor schools. According to the NAEP data, there were no substantial gains in mathematics after NCLB. In 1965, the Equality of Educational Opportunity Study of 1965 was a landmark event and had several sociologists who knew that the majority of the variance in school achievements lies within, not between, schools. The sociologists mostly observed the differences in achievements between schools.

This was actually explained by the characteristics of students and parents rather than by the position of schools. Thus, it is easy to mistake factors that are really associated with students, such as differences in family background, as those of schools. This study examines whether or not the NCLB law has affected school districts in New York City by decreasing those schools at the secondary level with poor performances in mathematics and low proficiency in English Language Arts (ELA).

The NCLB law of 2002 aimed to meet the goal of every child in public school to adequately have equal access to a high-quality education and increase the focus on failing schools and students who underperform (Coleman, 1990).

You Are What You Eat

Here is some need-to-know information for parents and learners when it comes to their eating habits and function in and out of the classroom: healthy eating. We talked about the brain in my previous book, "Anatomy of a Model Student" and know there are some more important items parents and learners are not aware of about their health that might impede upon their educational needs. There are several studies about how nutrition affects the brain and behavior. This research area is relatively new. Scientists are just coming around their findings and have yet to close in on definitive truth in understanding how changes in our kids' nutrition can alter the brain and cause changes that might lead to neurological defects, affect intelligence, mood, and the way we act. Those experiments with kids investigated how the balance of nutrition brain behavior interaction were first focused on effects of malnutrition, but looking at the behavior interaction is difficult for several reasons:

• *Poor nutrition and environmental issues can cause a change in behaviors. Education, social and family crises may also cause behavior issues.*

• *We looked at only one substance in our human diet. A particular vitamin or mineral can affect behavior. There are ethical factors like the Tuskegee Syphilis Experiment that disallow the testing on humans with particular nutrients and cannot be done, so many data come from animal testing. We do examine famine and starvation studies that focus on humans who lack nutrients.*

Humans respond to diets differently. Your body structure is a factor.

• *A change in your diet triggers what's called a placebo effect. An effect that people think something will occur in their diet will affect their behavior. The effect will often happen even if the nutrients are not causing the changes.*

• *The true definition of intelligence becomes controversial in the realm of nutrition-brain behavior. Some people will argue the fact that your IQ tests do not accurately measure intelligence if its effects are due to diet changes.*

Please understand that your brain acts similar to an automobile. A vehicle needs oil, power steering fluid, and other means to make it run efficiently. The average human brain also must have special needs to operate properly.

Your brain must have the following: glucose, minerals, vitamins, and other essentials that can give the needed fuel or energy to function properly. Glucose is the energy for your brain. To have it, you must eat proper foods, such as those with carbohydrates, that can be easily converted into glucose.

The brain must be able to manufacture the right fats, including proteins, to support the needed connections that develop routinely. This connection is called myelin, a fatty coating on your axons. This can happen once you eat proteins and fats that get digested with and by amino acids and fatty acids that produce the new brain fats and proteins. People, this is a very important process because without it, your brain will not function properly, and no building blocks can be developed to support a good brain function. Please understand that too little (deficiency) or too much (overloaded) of this nutrient can cause your nervous system to malfunction.

Now, in terms of fats or lipids, not all fats are bad for you. Your body contains both good and bad fats. Most are essential for your body and brain tissue. There are two lipids that are very important to the brain, namely, n-6 and n-3 fatty acids. If you suffer from low levels of n-3 fatty acids, it can affect your vision and may damage your retina. Other studies on animals showed low or no diet of n-3 fatty acids can cause learning, motivation, and motor issues that will taint your neurotransmitter dopamine and serotonin brain areas. The lack or low levels of n-6 fatty acids can affect your neurotransmitter and influence your ability to use glucose with neurons.

Parents, get a pencil or a pen. This is very important for you to know while your children are in school. There are certain foods that have nutrients that start up everything in the brain. We call them precursors for the neurotransmitters. If you have low levels of these precursors, your brain will not be able to function well enough to produce some neurotransmitters. The lack of nutrients can cause mental and neurological disorders or mishaps.

The following are some forms of neurotransmitters:

1. *Aspartic Acid – Used to make a separate or salty water-based form. It is found in peanuts, potatoes, eggs, and grains.*

2. *Choline – Used to make acetylcholine to help with nerve and muscle actions. It is found in eggs, liver, and soybean.*

3. *Glutamic Acid – Used to make glutamate, which is salt based. It is found in flour and potatoes.*

4. *Phenylalanine – Used to make dopamine that aids in movement and motion in the brain. Phenylalanine is a crystalline water soluble substance found in beets, soybeans, almonds, eggs, meat, and grains.*

5. *Tryptophan – Used to make serotonin. It is a colorless crystalline amino acid that is found in eggs, meat, skim milk, bananas, yogurt, and cheese.*

6. *Tyrosine – Used to make norepinephrine. It is also a crystalline amino acid essential for the development of the neurotransmitter norepinephrine that supports the central nervous system. It's found in milk, meat, fish, and legumes.*

The above precursors lead to a better mind and nerve base if incorporated into your everyday diet during the school day and beyond. You can look into these and much more than what I'm giving you, but it is important that you begin with the basics. You are what you eat, and the outcome can be to your advantage.

The end game in all of this is that your children will be able to understand what it takes to have a healthy mind and body, but the brain is the link to it all. Protect your mind and body and everything else will fall in place. (Here is a must to get and list: eat all and any purple fruit or vegetables like – grapes, plums, berries, nuts, black/blue cherries, and the like. These fruits that are purple help the brain grow and function superbly. Get it and eat it!) If you do not listen to your mind when it tells you it needs to be fed, you will see the results, and it will not be a pretty picture. Your brain needs to be fed the right foods to attain its peak performance. Many students fail to listen to their brains and lose out in making the best of a good healthy mind. You don't have to be wealthy to eat the right foods, and yes, it can be expensive, but there are foods that aren't costly. You just have to pay attention to the basics: fruits and veggies. You are what you eat, and we need to get back to the basics of living and living well. Remember this tip if you are taking an exam:

- *Drink a tall glass of water half an hour before an exam.*

- *Eat a banana forty-five minutes before an exam.*

- *Study a week before the exam, not the night before (only).*

- *Read the chapters or notes each day until the exam.*

- *The night before your exam, eat fish, veggies, blueberries, and/ or any green fruit.*

These are some of the tips I used and taught many of my former students. It works and keeps your mind sharp during and after the exam. In addition, if you do not exercise, you might want to in the midst of your daily routine. Exercise is important. You don't have to go to a gym and spend hundreds of dollars on equipment, but taking up a routine of just simply walking for thirty minutes or steadily moving in a repetitive pattern for thirty times a day will help you stimulate your body into staying in shape. Remember, your body is a machine and is designed to be in motion so all its moving parts are functioning well. Not everyone will agree, but think of your body being that same car we spoke about earlier; it still needs to move and function well in order to have you get the best of its performance. Another tip in the world of staying in shape is the idea of not letting time be wasted when you could be doing something productive. Case in point, we all had one time or another waited on a bank line or ticket booth line. How often do we ask, is it ever going to move fast enough toward the front? Well, this is a tip you could think about doing while waiting on the line. Begin to do tippy toe bends. Yes, I said stand on your toes. Up and down as you are waiting. This will help you build your calf muscles and keep your body in motion while you wait on the line. The brain can be stimulated also as you wait by playing a mind game. I did this many times while on the NYC subway holding on the straphanger bars. Look at the advertising posters and look at the words stretched out of each paragraph on the poster. What I did was I would count all letters that begin with whatever the first word I'm reading is showing. For example, if I saw the word people, I would begin to count how many times P is in that paragraph. I would move on to the next letter, E, and do the same thing until I'm done with all of the words. By that time, my stop would come up. This is just a way to keep your mind active. Of course it is better to have a book on hand while doing any of the locations mentioned if you are on a long line.

You and your Brain

Let's look at the human brain. The brain is a complex organ. Medical science is still learning so much about the brain that it's a fascinating subject just by itself. Whenever we think, learn, and/or remember things, there are groups of neurons that work over time to make sure we are doing the required tasks. Don't feel bad if you find yourself faced with hard attributes to concentrate on an academic subject. Thinking is not always easy, but the brain can make it look easy. It is a simple task once the neurons get to moving. These little guys work physically to accomplish whatever the task is being asked. If there is a difficult task or never before-seen subject flairs up, there are nearby neurons that join the group and begin to work on your behalf to get the job done. Training your brain can make this task much more reliable. Some call it rewiring the brain to strengthen its power to perform efficiently. I am guilty of telling thousands of students to always use your brain and not to be lazy. Not thinking is not good at all. Dr. John Ratey of Harvard Medical School cautions us to use our brains and work it; by not doing it is bad, but doing it keeps it vital and growing.

Let's take a short detour and learn what the brain is all about. Once this is better understood, we can say for sure that if you don't take care of yours, you will be in bad shape for now and forevermore. You were only given one brain, young folks; don't lose it to bad and unnecessary unproductive activities and drugs. Your brain was created with two types of cells, namely, neurons and glia. Neurons make up about 10 percent of those cells and glia 90 percent of brain cells. The neurons are what are so important to teachers and educators. These neuron cells are closely linked to learning. The neurons have a well-packed cell body, dendrites, and an axon.

Dendrites come from the Greek word dendron or "tree." Its shape is similar to a tree branch. Dendrites are projections of neurons that act to propagate the electrochemical stimulation received from other neural cells to the cell body. Axons are those nerve fibers that are long, slender projections of a nerve cell that conduct electrical impulses. Axons are the primary transmission lines of the nervous system. Together, these two partners work in harmony. Together they propel as they generate a constant firing of information throughout the brain.

Each time you begin to receive information; your dendrites begin to sprout all over your brain. With your experiences, from having a challenging exam (passing with 100 percent) to getting a new car after graduating, your brain gathers fresh information, and it causes your dendrites to bloom. This is the part that I call wriggles on the brain. New information is added to the brain area. When students are engaging and learning from the classroom and a great deal of information is being taught, thousands of dendrites are being sprouted from one neuron. Each neuron has its own axon to transmit information. Dendrites can receive information from other neighboring dendrites when connecting from a neuron axon. This is called a synaptic connection. A synaptic connection occurs when learning is evident. Creating a synaptic connection is causing tremendous wriggles on the brain. Hence, when neurons exchange information back and forth, learning occurs. Therefore, when you're learning to drive, bake cookies, play golf, and/ or write books, it all produces dendrites that build synaptic connections. Remember, in order to keep your mind sharp and brain functional to its highest levels you must feed it those purple colored fruits and veggies!

Have you ever asked yourself what is studying? Studying according to dictionary.com is defined as an application of the mind to the acquisition of knowledge, as by reading, investigation, or reflection. There are long hours of studying to get the best results and a completed trial. Another part of the definition is taking a look at might be or examines closely in order to observe or read.

As we progress in our journey to successful bliss of learning how to study and studying in its art form. Yes, let me be clear, it is an art. According to the dictionary art is a diverse range of human activities in creating visual, auditory or performing artifacts. One early sense of the definition of art is closely related to the older Latin meaning, which roughly translates to "skill" or "craft". Therefore, studying is duly noted as a complex art which requires skill. This is the key word, skill. In order to have skill you must pay attention to some rules that are in your best interest to accomplish your goal to achieve the best outcome. Yes, the best outcome. Not just any but an outcome in your perseverance will be developed but persevere. However, the best outcome is what you desire.

Studying, no matter what you must do and let it transpire into the best outcome! Before you begin your studying, always have a notebook next to you, on your desk. For most college students it is recommended that you spend at least two or more hours a week for each credit hour course you are taking. The utmost important task to remember whether you're in middle, high school or are in college there is some level of displaced freedom of independence that may stir you in the wrong direction in your studying habits if you are not careful.

The very fact that educators and experts say that 17 hours per week is needed to prepare for the course content, however, you must get into the frame of mind to prepare for the course work and you must be aware of what you eat and drink during the studying process.

Anyone can study and learn how to study without much effort. The problem I noticed in my research and experiences with thousands of students in the last 25 years is that many have very little patience and/or skills to go about studying to get the best outcome. It makes no sense to study for an half hour and expect to get a grade A when the subject of a math final covers 12 topics and you only know six, with few doubts you're going to do well. On the other hand, some may have that competitive edge to review quickly and be able to have much retained to have a greater outcome with little studying done, if there is such a thing as the few exceptions to the rule, however, many students lack patience.

In contrast, studying is not the same as doing homework. Too often I hear many students try to equate the two but they are not faintly the same. Please do understand and

learn the difference between doing homework and call yourself studying. You must learn how to approach each of these tasks. It does not matter whether you are a high school or college student you can learn and apply these five tips for effective studying. In addition, you can learn how factors such as your environment and expectation can affect your outcome for success while studying.

What's really behind the steps on how to read a textbook

Textbooks are necessary in all schools and training courses. No matter what the subject if you have been in any education forum, school or institution of learning, even a barn gathering with two or more individuals, it is almost necessary to have written materials on the subject that will require some reading. It is very important that you absorb and retain as much information as possible. Therefore, what is really behind the steps to reading a textbook as you're studying?

Here are a few eye openers you might want to use:

Step #1: Overview - *Before you begin your reading into the textbook take some time to get familiar with the textbook. Look at it, feel it, and hold it close to yourself. Really, do it, because you will be depending on its* *information to get you through the next exam successfully. Skim through the cover and read the title then go to all of the chapters and read those chapters (the titles) especially those that you are about to study. Read all of the headings and subheadings with introductions. Learn the author's name too. Take a notepad and jot down those words that are bold, italic, and have special reference markings. Jot down special terms.*

Step #2: What you don't know, ask. *You are never too old to forget how to develop questions based on what you learned during the overview step. Here is the time to ask yourself what the most important concepts or terms in the chapter are. You should always keep in mind a question is best asked when it's prepared like Who?, What?, When?, Where?, Why?, and How?. You can answer while you read.*

Step #3: What is fundamental? *– Once you have introduced yourself with the chapters of the textbook it is time to do the fundamental task of reading. Remember to have that bottle of water next to you while reading. No sugar beverage. Just a glass or bottle of water. As you read remember to go back to steps one and two and jot down key concepts and terms. I often use a bright highlighter (yellow) but use an orange highlighter for those bold terms that I will jot down on my notepad. In addition, if you noticed on your syllabus additional chapter pages given why not read ahead? This will give you an advantage when the instructor discusses further concepts in class. Reading ahead helps you to develop a good reading habit and you'll learn about emphasizing those challenging concepts further in the textbooks.*

Step #4: Say what? *– After you have finished reading your textbook chapters the next thing that should come to mind is to ask yourself, what didn't I understand? Did I understand it, say what? Textbooks are talking to you and you should be understanding what is being said. It is very important to review your notes and recite the information you learned from your reading. A good practice is to ask questions that are pinned down from the subject and you want to absorb as much as possible. To do this successfully you must review those terms, bold or italics with confidence. If you lack confidence, then it is wise to just reread the text or repeat steps 2 and 3.*

Step #5: Record your findings *– Now that you have accomplished the hard phase of your preparedness it is time to record what you learned from your reading. Write it down, write it down and yes write it down. Invest* in a notebook and a good pen that you can write smoothly and it feels good with your fingers and thumb. Really! Review those questions and answer your questions by seeking the facts and the facts only. Write those headings and label your notebook accordingly and remember this is for your review and understanding so you want to write as best you can so that you have the competitive edge when it is time to prepare for the test or exam. It is best to write down the terms and summaries on the subject. Each chapter you read should have a summary at the end. Reviewing it and writing down the highlights is very important.

Step #6: The end game review – *You have just completed your reading and now you are ready to review your notes and you should take those notes and review those points and facts that you have learned. Concentrate on the topic headings and subheadings. Keep that in your mind because in many cases an instructor may rely on that as a quick go to point of view to ask students in any exam, ie. questions on the subheading topics. Also please don't think it is necessary to write in pages from the textbook that you should read at a later time. Put that in your notebook.*

You must organize yourself!

I'm sure we have all heard the phrase, "First things first", but I like to change that to say, "Important things are first" to assure what is first gets the attention it needs in order to be successful first! If you want to study and do it well, you must first know your priorities and get the correct mind-set because if your mind is not in it you will fail at all costs.

The most important task to know and be certain of is the need to be organized. Always have a pencil or any writing utensil with you at all times during your studying period. Even in your regular class in school keep more than one writing tool on you. Make sure you take down the assignments or homework word for word. Never assume that your teacher has meant something totally different from class period. You could be on the wrong path while you are studying.

Secondly, I want to give you advice to make sure you don't lose your work or notes from class. Keep it, save it in your computer or disk but don't lose the assignments. Mostly, this advice is more for the college student than the high school students but keeping copies on a previous exam, quiz and/or reported notes is important.

Thirdly, make sure wherever you decide to have your studying spot or location make sure it is consistent and set up with all necessary supplies. Be organized! Some people will be critical at your designated area of studying but that should be ok with you because it is organized to what has made you comfortable to do the task. Don't change the settings. Keep all of your books and school supplies in the same places you designated. With all of the pens, pencils, dictionaries, notebooks, chrome book, etc., you need. Make sure no one moves your supplies and/or tools. Also, make sure you have a bottle of water nearby. You should always drink water and no juices while studying. Your brain must feed and absorb nutrients that are important to your task and juices, sodas and alcohol can derail your thinking and memory sensors.

This might be too farfetched in your thinking, but the brain and nerves go hand and hand when it comes to studying. There is a major nerve in the back of your head that is so important to your state of mind and growth that learning more about it will be useful to your studying habits. It is an essential nerve called the vagus nerve. The vagus nerve is the longest and most difficult nerve to comprehend, it is one of 12 pairs of the cranial nerves in the brain. Its job is to transmit information from the brain to the surface of the body and to specific tissues and organs.

According to Webster's book of definitions, Vagus comes from the Latin term for "wandering" mostly because the vagus nerve enters organs throughout the neck, chest, stomach. It is also known as 10th cranial nerve or cranial nerve X.

To make this subject more understandable, the vagus nerve has a bunch of sensory nerve cells and is made up of two bunches of sensory nerve cell bodies connecting the brain stem to the body. This nerve allows the brain to monitor and receive information about a few of the body's different functions. It was said that there are multiple nervous systems but their functions are controlled by the vagus nerve and its related parts. In a nutshell, the vagus nerve promotes the autonomic nervous system, which consists of the parasympathetic and sympathetic parts.

The vagus nerve has a number of different functions. The four key functions of the vagus nerve are:

- *Sensory: From the throat, heart, lungs, and abdomen.*

- *Special sensory: Provides taste sensation behind the tongue.*

- *Motor: Provides movement functions for the muscles in the neck responsible for swallowing and speech.*

- *Parasympathetic: Responsible for the digestive tract, respiration, and heart rate functioning.*

The human body's nervous system is very unique. It can be divided into two areas: sympathetic and parasympathetic. You might ask, what does that have to do with me studying and who cares about a vagus nerve? Ok, my point is that the vagus nerve has these two remarkable sides:

- *The sympathetic side*

- *increases alertness, energy, blood pressure, heart rate, and breathing rate.*

- *The parasympathetic side*

- *The parasympathetic side, which the vagus nerve is heavily involved in, decreases alertness, blood pressure, and heart rate, and helps with calmness, relaxation, and digestion.*

For the purposes of this study guide I want you to focus on the sympathetic side of the vagus nerve. You must increase alertness, energy, breathing rate, and etc. The vagus nerve becomes a very important function in this studying process if you allow it. In addition, the vagus nerve communicates between the brain and your stomach. Information from the stomach to the brain and the reverse. Hence, the phrase - "gut feelings or go with your gut".

Relaxation helps with deep breathing as the vagus nerve communicates with your diaphragm. If you did the techniques mentioned earlier in this book with breathing and deep breathing, you can feel more relaxed. The vagus nerve decreases inflammation. It sends an anti-inflammatory signal to various parts of the body.

Are you listening...or just hearing?

Out of all the senses in the body, the sense of hearing is the most intriguing in my opinion because once you hear things it triggers an alert throughout the whole body to come alive to act. The first sound a baby hears in his mother's womb allows it to react to the notion of protection and comfort that it will survive, live and be taken care of without fear of the unknown. Once we hear for the first time and then thereafter, we are confident that the other senses fall in place to claim their perspective task and perform accordingly. To the contrary, listening requires a more in tune task. You must be able to tap into your keen sense of responsibility to focus on the task at hand and learn to follow instructions as they are given. Some may say this is like meditation. It requires concentration with a focus that cannot be broken. Your thoughts must be in line with the promise that your goal to complete the task can be attainable after following instructions.

Here is an exercise you can practice:

- *Find the smallest room in your house and bring a chair. If it happens to be your closet make sure you can sit inside, turn out the lights and sit against the wall that is pointed in the east direction of the house where you live.*

- *Sit down and face that wall. Close your eyes and listen to the sounds you hear as you turn your head towards the right side and then the left with eyes still closed.*

- *Sitting there with closed eyes begin to listen to the sounds and count how many different sounds you can recognize.*

- *As you sit there and have counted the number of different sounds then begin to count how many times you hear the same sounds.*

- *Lastly, open your eyes and turn the lights back on and take three deep breaths, rub your hands together and drink a tall glass of water.*

One of the most important things to do in any classroom or institution of learning is allowing the use of one of your major senses of the body be used effectively. The sense of Hearing – is the sense that causes you to perceive or become aware of things by the ear; to have the capacity of perceiving sound.

Now to briefly recap. Now you know how to get organized the next thing you want to focus on is having the transfer of information from your teacher in the class to your mind. During class lessons, it is best to engage in "active listening". Active listening is when you eliminate any and all distractions, and actually understand and can concentrate on what your teacher is saying. There is a difference between hearing what your professors or teacher says, and actively listening to what you actually hear.

Are you listening or just hearing me?

Active listening is when you can eliminate any and all distractions, and actually understand and can concentrate on what your teacher is saying. There is a difference between hearing what your professors or teacher says, and actively listening to what you actually hear.

This needs to be repeated. Active listening is just that as I stated, active. Key words are active and listening. According to the dictionary, being active requires engaging or being ready to engage in physically energetic pursuits. In addition to that definition: active - pursuing an occupation or activity at a particular place or in a particular way. Once again, we find ourselves emerging with the senses. The sense of touch, sight and audio. Touch, due to the fact you must have your notebook to write things down. Sight becomes important to see who is talking and aid in the learning process to watch body language and emotional display with your actions and reactions. Hearing is the final sense to seal the deal. It adds to comprehending the content and in most cases whether truly understood or not but the hearing is just the point of contact to secure the attempt to comprehend. The pieces that need to be glued are your abilities to concentrate and submit yourselves to your wills to understand lessons. Assessments and practices come hand in hand. The other important piece here is the extended thought of when you can eliminate any and all distractions. This is the very fiber that has caused many to bomb out on exams, fail to study successfully and/or just quit early on because they just can't get past this fact about eliminating distractions.

The ability to concentrate is not as easy as some think just because you are alone in a room with books and supplies in hand. It is altogether another struggle for many students to overcome.

Being in a noisy house or school trying to do the right thing in preparing for an exam is hard to accomplish but there are cases where students are by themselves and just get stuck in the room in the midst of quietness and lose all thoughts, comprehension and still can't concentrate! What can you do about that problem? Some Psychologists may call it cacophony of disturbing thoughts until we collapse at our day's end, but please keep in mind I'm no Psych-man but I do understand that we must be true to ourselves and learn about ourselves moving forward. You should get to know YOU! If you find yourself alone and trying to get to a deep concentration of your very being before trying to study, keep in mind that if negative things and thoughts bother you don't go to a hidden place of quietness and think you don't like yourself. I don't want you to think, "I don't like ME." Please, this is not the time to get off the path. Your goal is looking for a quiet place to study to keep out the distractions. Therefore, a point of view, you should say to yourself, "I don't like this." Keep yourself always focused on the prize. The prize is being alone to eliminate distractions that keep you preoccupied and away from completing your schoolwork. Make a schedule and make sure you have access to that quiet place at all times or during your quiet time.

Not everyone has the patience or the strong will to do what is necessary to succeed, but you all have the potential to do well and to make yourselves very proud. Remember, no one knows you better than you so make the best you possible. If you want the best just be the best. Go for what you want and succeed with all the best intentions possible. Do not quit or give up the desire to succeed. Quitting comes internally first then gets acted upon by just being committed to the action. Don't do it. Everything comes to your thoughts whether good or bad. Emotions get ramped up at times and we go for it. Sadness, happy places or anger all come to mind but we have split seconds in most cases to act. This takes energy. I say, reserve that energy for a positive moment that gives you the opportunity to do something meaningful and powerful. This could be the chance you've been waiting for and the time has come to act in a positive way. However, you could easily mess it up or blow it away if you just quit! Remember the phrase, "quitters never win and winners never quit". I say a quitter never wins because they have no time to win because they are always quitting, and winners have no time to quit because they are constantly winning. Be on the winning side.

Studying and it's processing is not hard to do but requires a person to be consistent and make sure the tips and concepts described in this book are followed to make the best effort forward. Nothing can be truer than to hear someone say they didn't do well because of something or someone.

Do not hold others responsible for actions that you could avoid yourself. The most important thing to do in this case is to get up and do! Procrastination is the most common practicing fallback students are faced with today. It is hard to be freed if you have been in the clutches for such a long time but one must break loose before the mind gives up on any final attempts to break away.

Procrastination means having to act or the action of delaying or postponing something. How many of you are guilty of this action? According to a New York Times article, (Smarter-living), the statement read stated why we procrastinate and it has nothing to do with self-control. The article stated that procrastination is nothing more than how you cope with your challenging emotions and negative moods induced by certain things you do or tasks. (Lieberman, 2019). Some would say it's all about how lazy you are and you just don't care at that moment, but it's not.

Keep in mind, procrastination is a word derived from the Latin word *procrastinare* which means to put off until tomorrow. Now, wait just one moment. How many of you have said that and really wait until tomorrow to do what was meant to do then and now? This strange word, procrastination is also derived from the ancient Greek word *akrasia* - meaning doing something against our better judgement. Too often, the Greeks find a better or appropriate way to convey words into full meaning and our English language translates it into deep robust meaning. However, the fact that this is more than a task, but a task based on emotions of the negative kind.

Summarizing what we have learned: There are habits that we grew up with that made us who and what we have become. So, you think you know how to study? This book was written and inspired from a high school teacher who asked me to compile some of my workshops, lessons and tips from years of training and assisting students with their study habits and test strategies.

Studying is a chore. You can't escape the fact it's part of the academia and is essential.

References

Bennett, Tyrone, L. *Anatomy of a Model Student. Xlibris, LLC.* (Sept. 2015)

College (August 2014). *Article.www.usatoday.com*

Jaffee, David, *Stop Telling Students to Study for exams.* (April 22, 2012). *Article. www.Chronicle.com*

Jimenz, Laura, Sargrad, Scott, Morales, Jessica and Thompson, Maggie. *The cost of Catching up.* (Sept. 28, 2016) *.www.americanprogress.org*

How-much-do-college-students-really-study? (May, 2016). https://inforefuge.com

Kruger, Susan. *How to Study,* (2018). www.resaerchgate.net/publication-228786091. 2009-2013

Smart-living. (March 25, 2019). https://www.nytimes.com

Stop Telling Students to Study.(April 22, 2012). Article.131622. www. chronicle.com

The Art of Studying more Efficiently, (October 16, 2013). https://ualr.edu/ blackboard

13-reasons college students don't know study. (May 12, 2017). https:// blog.4tests.com

What is the reason that students don't study well? (February 10, 2017). https://www.quora.com

Why do we force students to study for hours instead of encouraging them to actually practice the material? https://www.quora.com

CPSIA information can be obtained
at www.ICGtesting.com
Printed in the USA
BVHW081638210721
612419BV00005B/416